STAR VIKINGS

VIKINGS, WHALES AND COFFEE

by
DR PETER STARBUCK

Copyright ©PeterStarbuck2022
All rights reserved.
ISBN: 9798408521548
Copyright ©PeterStarbuck2022

Dedicated to family, friends and to all those who gave such great encouragement in researching and completing this book.

CONTENTS

Chapter 1	Overview	7
Chapter 2	Peter and Heather Starbuck's Interest	11
Chapter 3	Scientific Research	15
Chapter 4	The Vikings	19
Chapter 5	The New World Starbucks	25
Chapter 6	The Nantucket Starbucks and the Birth of Whaling	31
Chapter 7	The Quaker Connection	33
Chapter 8	'The Three Brothers'	35
Chapter 9	The Decline of Whaling	39
Chapter 10	The Milford Haven Starbucks	41
Chapter 11	Benjamin Franklin and Nantucket	45
Chapter 12	How Coffee Came out of Nantucket	57
• Folgers		57
• Starbucks		59
Chapter 13	Conclusions	63

Appendix i   65
- University of Leicester
- Seeking Viking Descendants in the North of England
- 'What's in a name?'

Appendix ii   (Herbert) Peter Starbuck genealogy   67

Appendix iii   69
- Family Crests
- Starbuck's American Coats of Arms

Bibliography   71
About the Author Dr Peter Starbuck   73

DR PETER STARBUCK

CHAPTER 1

OVERVIEW

The general belief was that Christopher Columbus was the first to discover America while looking for India in 1492. This was common knowledge taught in schools in the 1950's.

The current perception is that the Siberians were America's original human settlers. They travelled from Siberia across the Bering Straits into Alaska to became North America's indigenous population.

By the 17th century the English began to take interest in America, particularly those of *The Mayflower Generation* who were disturbed by events at home and in Europe.

It would be happenings of over a century earlier that would prompt these early settlers to leave their British homelands.

One of the most destructive events in history with eight million deaths, the 30 Year European War of Christian religious conflict saw empires extended and various Christian creeds imposed.

With the war concluding, as the head of the Catholic Church, the Pope would not endorse the Tudor King of England Henry XIII's wish to divorce. To this Henry named himself head of the Christian Church in Britain, which separated as the Anglican Church.

This period known as the Reformation progressed from 1517 to 1648, with continued conflict within the Catholic Church, and with Martin Luther being the most conspicuous critical intellectual.

King Henry XIII's separation was confirmed as Puritans and Quakers (non-conformists) emerged and continued under his daughter Queen Elizabeth I, the *Virgin Queen* who remained single and died without an heir in 1603.

The prospect was that the Stuarts would take the throne and revert to Catholicism. This caused great insecurity for the non-conformists. They were greatly concerned an established Anglican Church had not gone far enough in separating from Rome under the Tudors.

Thus their plan of action was to leave England for the New World of America. Funds were soon raised to buy provisions and engage a crew for *The Mayflower*.

First attempting to sail from Southampton on the 5th August 1620, then from Dartmouth on the 21st August 1620, *The Mayflower* finally set sail from Plymouth, England, on the 16th September 1620. With one hundred and two passengers and a crew of nearly thirty, all were bound for New England, America to start a new life.

With their first half of the voyage taken on calm seas and beneath clear skies the luck of fine weather took a turn for the worse.

Continuous north-easterly storms battered *The Mayflower*. With ocean swells rising to over a hundred feet huge waves constantly crashed across the ships topside deck. Passengers were forced to remain below deck in darkness as powerful waves tossed their ship about in different directions, cold sea water soaking everyone and everything above and below *The Mayflower's* wooden decks.

There would be only one fatality during the settler's Atlantic voyage. During one storm a servant of the respected physician Samuel Fuller died and was ceremoniously buried at sea, however within the midst of another storm a child was born and was poignantly christened Oceanus Hopkins.

Towards the final few weeks of *The Mayflower's* journey those aboard met with a storm so fierce that the ship's sails could not be used. It was feared strong gale force winds would inevitably play so hard across her sails that *The Mayflower* would risk losing her three masts - the mizzen (aft), the main (midship), and the fore mast.

After being exposed to the elements and battling through Atlantic tempests for close to ten weeks *The Mayflower* reached America and dropped anchor near the tip of Cape Cod, Massachusetts, on the 21st November 1620.

As a consequence of delays in preparations and inadequate stores *The Mayflower's* passengers soon discovered they had arrived at the wrong time of the year to grow crops, the provisions brought with them proving more than inadequate.

It was reported that these early settlers were too lazy to work themselves and began stealing corn and animals from the North American indigenous population (Native Americans/North American Indians) who owned the land.

Once the first immigrants had settled more ships arrived from England. Carrying smallpox aboard, the disease proved more virile to America's indigenous population who did not hold the same immune system as the Europeans.

Where some settlement towns were developing in ways of law and order as more settlers arrived, other towns remained in a state of chaos. In 1633 the first war broke out between settlers and Native Americans at Hartford. The settlers would have been defeated if the Narragansett tribe had not been loyal to them.

One of the fundamental issues was that numerous indigenous American tribes which included the Uncas, Narragansett, Pequots, Mohegan, Mohicans, Mohawks and the Wampanoag, owned the land but had no commercial knowledge compared to English settlers from more developed communities. This resulted in said tribes selling large tracks of land for axes, bells and rifles.

Some were cooperative with the settlers whereas others waged guerrilla war by burning fields and farms and annihilating forts. The conflict between them became known as the 30 Year King Philip War - the title of the re-named Native American who did not want peace. Male natives not killed by war were murdered by the English Army, while females and children were sold as slaves to the West Indies.

Eventually the war ended in 1677 with the settlers defeating the indigenous Americans. The settlers then went on to sell one thousand indigenous men to the West Indies. The war wiped out ten percent of New England's settlers and half of the American indigenous population.

Alongside the war in New England, America, England was also in conflict at home within England's Civil War. With King Charles I crowned in 1625 he remained at rule until losing to Oliver Cromwell and was beheaded in 1649.

England's conflicts continued when in 1652 there was a trade war with Holland, and friction with France remained ever present. On a religious front, from 1649 Anglican Christianity including the non-conformists prevailed until 1660 when the King Charles II restored Catholicism.

Records show that when the settlers arrived in Cape Cod it was occupied by the Wampanoag tribe who welcomed their new visitors. Mention was also recorded about Benjamin Franklin, one of the world's most accomplished humans in any century.

One of America's founding fathers, Franklin's mother was a Foulger (also written as Folger) who settled on Cape Cod's Nantucket Island, as did the Starbucks, with whom the Foulgers intermarried.

CHAPTER 2

PETER AND HEATHER STARBUCK'S INTEREST

Against its history of conflict, in late summer 1987, with my wife Heather we booked a three week car drive discovery holiday in New England, America.

Beginning in Boston, we set off north through Maine and across the St. Lawrence River into Canada. We then re-entered America at Niagara Falls. Returning southwards through New England we at last arrived at Hyannis Port on the south coast of Cape Cod. It was here Nantucket Island was pointed out to us.

A small island thirty miles south of Cape Cod, Massachusetts, Nantucket Island is seen as a summer destination where visitors gather on its white sand beaches and dunes; a luxury playground where Boston's elite escape to in order to avoid their city's stuffy summers. The piers and cobblestone streets of Nantucket Town are lined with restaurants, high-end boutiques and churches. The town is also home to a Whaling Museum recounting Nantucket Island's role as a 19th century hub for America's once prosperous whaling industry.

The Nantucket Whaling Museum incorporates exhibition space connecting the 1847 Hadwen & Barney Oil and Candle Factory, and the 1971 Peter Foulger Museum. Suspended from the ceiling a forty-six-foot-long sperm whale skeleton greets the museum's visitors.

The Hadwen & Barney Oil and Candle Factory exhibit explains the complicated process of refining whale oil and the making of spermaceti candles, just one of a multitude of Nantucket industries that came about from the whaling era.

We were told that with the name of Starbuck we should take the local ferry and visit Nantucket island. Locals further explained the family name of Starbuck had long been associated with this region, in particular with the Nantucket whaling industry of the 17th and 19th centuries.

Intrigued by such accounts we duly followed up their recommendation. We were both amazed by what we found.

We soon discovered the Starbuck name and the early whaling industry of Nantucket were bonded. It was encouraging to find the island's locals were very knowledgeable about these early Starbucks.

There were records for the island going back to the mid-17th century with Edward Starbuck named as an early settler among the first band of landowners.

Walking through Nantucket Town, we noticed three conspicuously large houses on the town's Main Street. These magnificent town houses were built by Joseph Starbuck specifically for his three sons William, Matthew and George.

As a professional builder I at once noticed a distinctive feature of these houses; that they are built of brick.

As Heather and I were to find out later with similar structures on the Falkland Islands, this was once a status symbol in areas that did not have any deposits of brick clay. The owners were displaying they could afford to import brick from far away.

Edward Starbuck (1604–1690) and his Welsh-born wife Catherine Reynolds (sometimes spelt Katherine) had originally emigrated further along the coast to Dover in New Hampshire, America, from Derbyshire, England in 1635.

The American city of Dover has a long history spanning nearly four centuries.

Early days as a colonial seaport led to the city's successful shipbuilding industry in the 1700's, which flourished in the 19th century as the nation's leading manufacturer of cotton goods.

First settled by Puritan Europeans in 1623, Dover, soon developed into a thriving settlement with Edward Starbuck becoming a man of stature within this community. However, contemporary records indicate that Edward was, or became, an Anabaptist and thus fell foul to an overbearing Puritan governance.

This eventually saw him moving his family to Nantucket Island in 1648, a place which was quickly developing into a Quaker community.

Once again Edward became a leading light in the community after purchasing a one-twentieth share of land offered up for sale to ten families and their partners.

He was also commissioned by the Wampanoag tribe to settle any internal disputes. It is believed the Wampanoag tribe have lived in south-eastern Massachusetts for more than 12,000 years.

Through Edward's leadership it was seen that all living on Nantucket Island did so compatibly throughout the outside world's consistent waring period.

Leaving the island with this knowledge Heather and I reflected on what an interesting discovery it had been.

As more information came to light it became apparent that an interesting story was awaiting discovery.

Intermittently the story unfolded as we found books on Nantucket whaling - most of which made reference to the Starbucks.

Nantucket Whale Flags

One of particular reference to the Starbucks was a survey of Mercantile House flags (8 Funnels 1979 JL Loughran) - published by Waine Research, Wolverhampton, England, who gave permission to reproduce the Starbuck Flags as seen below.

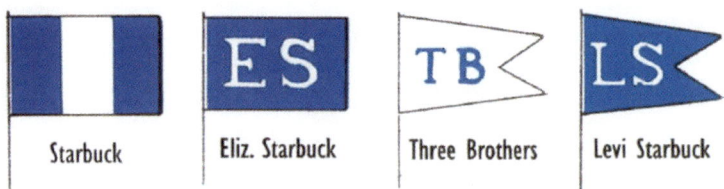

The definitive record of Nantucket Whale Flags establishes that the Starbuck flags are blue and white.
 The flag labelled 'Starbuck' is the house flag. The three others are Starbuck ship flags.

In 2007 I was approached by the first of several professional genealogists who wanted to research the Starbuck name and plot a family tree.
 It was then that the first of several unpredictable events occurred.

CHAPTER 3

SCIENTIFIC RESEARCH
INHERITED GENES/HAPLOGROUPS

In 2009 the University of Leicester, Department of Genetics received a grant from the British Government to conduct a survey into selected old North of England surnames to determine who had Viking ancestry.

The research was conducted by Professors Mark A. Jobling and Turi King. Professor Turi King was the expert who later identified Richard III bones found below the tarmac of a car park in Leicester in 2012.

They employed a methodology that included obtaining genetic data from DNA samples of specifically identified participants.

DNA or Deoxyribonucleic acid, is a molecule composed of two polynucleotide chains, these chains coil around each other to form a double helix, this carries genetic instructions for the development, functioning, growth and reproduction of all known organisms, and many viruses.

DNA samples were analysed to identify the most likely geographical origins of the participants, and so revealing their ethnicity and correspondence with historical records.

The academic aim concentrated on mapping the distribution of people with these surnames around the world at different times in history.

In the northern hemisphere, the Norsemen, or Vikings as they are now popularly called were the master-mariners of their era around 7th century AD.

Sailing vast distances by sea they almost certainly reached the shores of North America nearly 800 years before the Columbus voyage of 1492.

Holding an extremely aggressive warrior culture gave them many conquests in a period termed the '*Viking era*', but there was another aspect to their character, they were traders and farmers too, forming settlements across many parts of the world's northern hemisphere, Northern England included.

I was one of the individuals contacted because 'Starbuck' was on the list of names for their study of Viking ancestry in the North of England. I agreed to participate in the study and provided a sample of my own DNA.

On completion of the research programme I received a detailed report from the University explaining their findings and indicating the origins of my family name.

Their DNA analysis revealed my family origins were in a particular area of Scandinavia.

Professor King explained that individuals sharing a common surname, but who are not currently close relatives, could well have had a common ancestor several hundred years ago.

Forensic DNA typing enables the identification of these distant relatives through a component of human DNA termed the 'Y' chromosome.

As for surnames, a son inherits this chromosome from his father and all men sharing the surname of a common ancestor will have this 'Y' chromosome in their DNA, provided, of course, a legitimate lineage exists.

Haplogroups – Starbuck genes - Y chromosome Results

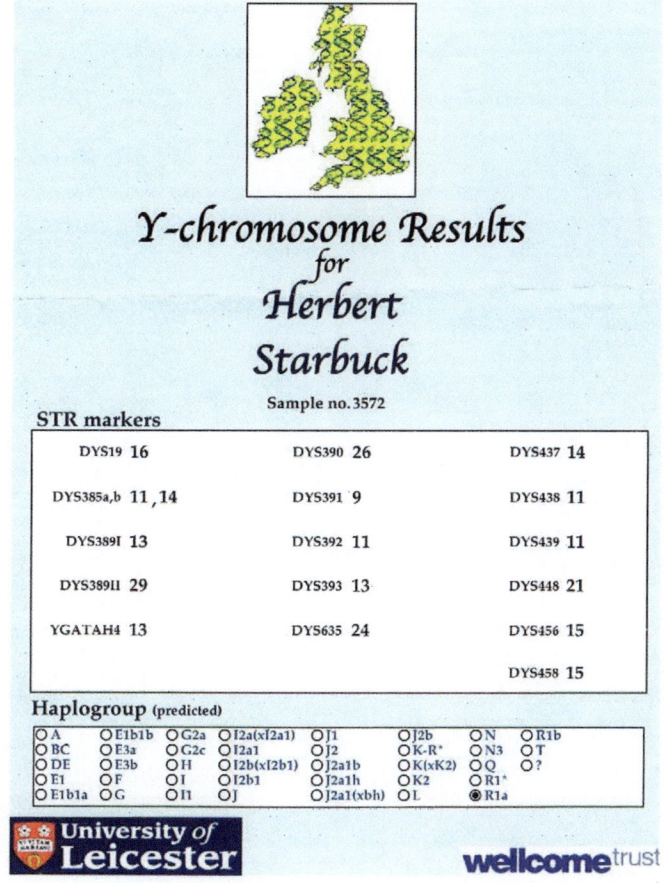

A haplogroup classifies a genetic population of people sharing a common ancestor through their 'Y' chromosome.

The university study team determined that the haplogroup I belong to is the R1a group which is quite rare in Britain; only about 5 per cent of the population share it.

In Western Europe the dominant haplogroup is R1b1b2, the major haplogroup for the British Isles, Norway, Denmark, Sweden, Holland, Germany and France.

Haplogroup diversity in Europe

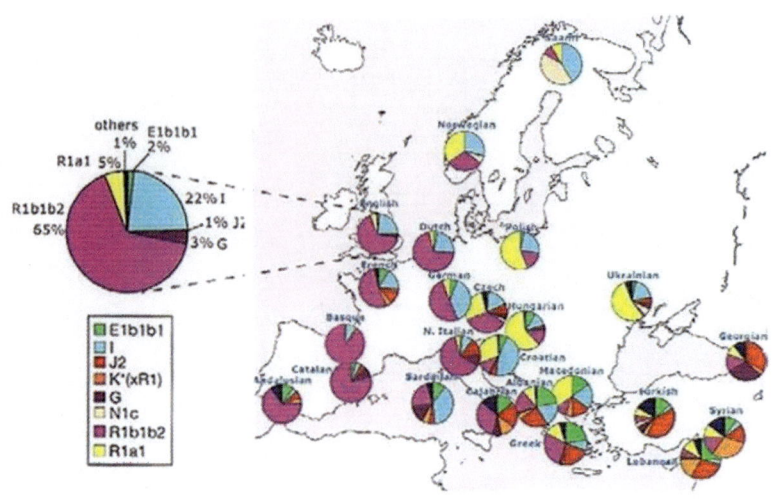

The R1a haplogroup is:

"Generally quite rare in Britain except in regions with strong Norse ancestry regarded as a signature of Norse Viking ancestry and common (26%) in Norway. It is also found at high frequencies in Central Europe and India."

Leicester University

Along with a copy of my 'Y' chromosome results, I received the following commentary from the study team:

"Vikings and Norsemen from Scandinavia, comprising Demark, Norway and Sweden, arrived on the coast of North East England. They first arrived in their longboats across the North Sea to attack Lindisfarne Monastery In 793AD, they attacked Jarrow and then Tynemouth in 800AD.

Within a relatively short period of time they settled in England, as proven by discovered archaeological artefacts and remaining place names."

CHAPTER 4

THE VIKINGS

The 'Viking Age' in Great Britain lasted from around 793 AD until ending abruptly in 1066 AD with the Norman Invasion.

In the northern hemisphere Scandinavian Norsemen known as the Vikings were the foremost sailors of their era.

It is noted by the world's leading academics on seafaring that the Vikings reached the shores of North America in the late 10th century, a good five hundred years before Italian explorer and navigator Christopher Columbus discovered the Americas and the *'New World'* aboard his ship the Santa Maria in 1492 AD.

The Vikings were to arrive onto American soil for the first time after sailing from Greenland, a land they had conquered after colonising Iceland.

Records show that the first of the Vikings to reach America was Leif Eriksson the Norse explorer who is believed to have led the first European expedition to North America across the Atlantic Ocean.

The insight of the Vikings being the first arrivals onto American shores contradicts what was regularly taught in schools in the 1940's that - *'In 1492 Columbus sailed the ocean blue'* and discovered America.

Viking maritime skills were founded on their mastery of the art of boat construction. These skills of producing sturdy seafaring boats evolved at its fastest rate between 760 and 1000 AD.

Their *longboats* were constructed from ash trees and cut into broad planks; the Vikings were known as the Ascomanni (*"ash men"*) by the Germans.

The planks were laid using the *lapstrake* method of overlapping rough-sawn planking to produce an extremely flexible hull. This allowed these Viking longships to withstand the stresses and strains encountered on far ocean voyages.

Mastering the art of smelting iron ore to produce nails used in building ships, the Vikings hot-dipped these nails in oil to give a degree of resistance to a sea's salt-water corrosion.

With these shallow-draft vessels they sailed down Europe's major rivers and across the North Sea where they could beach their boats to mount surprise attacks.

Vikings were pagans and worshipped their own warlike gods. Feared as ruthless raiders, during this era they attacked and destroyed early Christian sites, plundering buildings and massacring all living there.

These warriors were not literate so their culture relied on a word-of-mouth transfer of knowledge. This was done mainly through sagas or great stories told around campfires.

The Norsemen's only attempt at producing physical records was in a symbolic method called runes.

Viking runes were a literal alphabet and believed to hold great power. Symbolising qualities and values associated with magic, runes were often scribed onto single stones and were utilised for divination and oracle reading purposes.

It would be the monks who encountered Viking attacks that recorded the exploits of these raiders in English written word.

Another aspect of these fierce Vikings was their penchant for trading. Evidence of this can be found in excavated sites across the British mainland, Iceland, Europe, and well into the Mediterranean.

In one British archaeological excavation a coin was discovered with both Christian and runic symbols impressed on it. This suggests a level of integration of cultures. Eventually, as the centuries advanced the Vikings would leave their beliefs of gods and goddesses, with Valhalla being their selected heaven, a place where only heroes went. In time they converted to Christianity, a faith discovered within the lands they had once been so intent on ransacking.

As accomplished sailors they navigated by following coastlines where possible. They also sailed over open water.

Out of sight of land, Viking sailors were expert at reading 'extended landfall' signs such as seabird sightings, cloud formations and patterns of wind and tide.

Viking laws governing their settlements were well defined. Those who committed serious crimes were often punished by banishment from their community.

Viking sagas tell the story of Erik Thorvaldsson, known as Erik the Red, who was expelled for three years from Iceland for unlawfully killing another man.

Erik and his band left Iceland in their longships and sailed westward. Discovering Greenland they became the first European settlers there.

It would be Erik's son and heir, Leif Eriksson who first landed on the North American coast.

He would go on to name the country *Vinland* after the wild grapevines found there.

At an archaeological site first excavated in the 1960's at L'Anse aux Meadows on the tip of Newfoundland's Great Northern peninsula, a Viking-style settlement was uncovered where artefacts including a bronze cloak pin, iron nails and rivets were found. This proved the first known evidence of a European presence in the Americas. A longhouse foundation was also revealed and more importantly a smelting furnace with remnants of clinker with iron in it.

The carbon dating of structures and artefacts found at L'Anse aux Meadows estimate to be dated from 990 to 1050 AD.

In 793 AD the Vikings attacked Lindisfarne, a designated holy island just off the Northumbrian coast of England to the west of the North Sea.

Lindisfarne's church of St. Cuthbert and its surrounding monastic grounds were taken by surprise as the Vikings proceeded to loot the monastery and either killed or enslaved many of the monks found there.

The assault on Lindisfarne was seen as attacking the sacred heart of the Northumbrian kingdom, thereby desecrating the exact location where Christian religion in Great Britain began. A place where St. Cuthbert (d. 687) had been bishop, and where his body was now revered as that of a saint.

Being the first time the Vikings had attacked a monastic site in Britain the attack was a major shock to medieval Christians.

The pillaging and slaughter on Lindisfarne proved only the beginning of the Viking's dominance on British soil.

The events of 793 AD marked the start of what is now termed the Viking Age, succeeding the Anglo-Saxons who had themselves the Romans.

As the Vikings became established they eventually built settlements, with York becoming their principal town in 873 AD, and farming becoming the main source of food.

Despite a particularly aggressive warrior culture an often overlooked fact is that the majority of these people were peaceful settlers in search of land to farm.

Many towns and cities around the UK confirm their Viking origins. This can be seen in British cities such as Durham, Nottingham, Stanford and Lincoln.

The Viking Age in Britain ended in 1066 AD with the Norman Invasion, but not with their total influence, as the Normans themselves were of Viking descent.

One of the contrasts of the Norman Invasion was that they would maintain Christianity as the British religion.

Today there are Viking sites across Europe.

The British towns of Derby, Grimsby, Rugby and Whitby are examples of Viking settlements, this is recognised in the fact that any town ending in *'by'* proves to have once been a Viking community; *'by'* is taken from the Old Norse and means *'farmstead'* or *'village'*. This can also be seen in the towns of Brondby and Lyngby in Denmark.

Another example of once Viking settlements is where *'thorpe'* is used at the end of a town's name, such as Scunthorpe, with *'thorpe'* meaning *'outlying farm'*.

In Yorkshire alone there are two hundred and ten *'by'* places and one hundred and fifty-five *'thorpes'*.

THE DERBYSHIRE STARBUCKS

In medieval Britain, the Starbuck name appeared most commonly in those counties where the Vikings had gained control. This was known as *'Daneland'*.

Danelaw was the part of England in which the laws of the Danes held sway.

Danelaw roughly comprised of fifteen shires: Leicester, York, Nottingham, Derbyshire, Lincoln, Essex, Cambridge, Suffolk, Norfolk, Northampton, Huntingdon, Bedford, Hertford, Middlesex, and Buckingham.

With the Starbuck name coming from within the heart of Daneland, an Old Norse description of a great river, *'Stor-Bokki'* appears in the Doomsday Book of 1086 as *'Starbok'*.

The village of *Starbeck* near Harrogate, Yorkshire, had the original name of *'Starbok'*, so called after the river running through it.

This evidence points towards the true origin of the Starbuck name.

Relevant to the above is the research of my 2007 professional genealogist and the discovery of my direct male lineage.

A remarkable ancestry that extends back over four hundred years to Edward Starbuck (b. 1604) in Derbyshire, England.

CHAPTER 5

THE NEW WORLD STARBUCKS

In 1635 Edward Starbuck left his home in Derbyshire to settle in the New World.

Seeking a new life, many of these early pilgrims held Calvinist religious beliefs. The family joined an established community in Dover, New Hampshire, which was recorded as being Anabaptist.

As opposed to being baptised as an infant, Anabaptists are Christians who believe in delaying baptism until they confesses their undying faith in Christ.

Direct descendants of the movement of Anabaptism are the Amish, Hutterites and the Mennonites.

Records from the time indicate that Edward ultimately became a stalwart citizen of the town.

Identifying Edward's growing influence and popularity among Dover's townsfolk the Puritan elite eventually challenged Edward's standing, having already established themselves in positions of power within the settlement.

With Anabaptists and Quakers stating the church should be distinct from the state, this view put them in conflict with the opposing views of Puritan groups.

In view of this the Puritan-dominated communities isolated the Anabaptists and Quakers.

In an act of an insular and inward looking thinking, the Puritans passed laws forbidding citizens from associating with those whose beliefs were grounded in Anabaptism and Quakerism.

The account reproduced below is of Edward's trials at the hands of these Puritans found in the provincial papers of the New Hampshire Historical Society:

Edward Starbuck, was born in 1604, in Derbyshire and died February 4th 1690-91. He came to America about 1635, from Derbyshire, England, bringing with him his wife, Katherine. He settled in Dover, New Hampshire, where he is first mentioned, June 30th 1643, when he received a grant for forty acres of land on each side of the Fresh River at Cutchechoe, and one plat of marsh above Cutchechoe Great Marsh.

Richard Walderne, Edward Colcord, Edward Starbuck, and William Furber. also received other grants of land at different times, including one of the marsh in Great Bay in 1643, one of the mill privilege at Cutchechoe Falls (with Thomas Wiggin), and one of timber to "accommodate" in 1650, and various others. He was one of the foremost settlers of Dover, a representative of the town in 1643 and 1646, and undoubtedly would have lived comfortably there until his death, honoured and respected by his fellow townsmen, he had not embraced the Baptist faith. He was the owner of extensive properties, and was in all probability a man of substance as to possessions, as tradition says he was in born. Despite this, he fell in disrepute for daring to differ in faith from the intolerant Puritans of his day.

"October 18th 1648 - The Court being informed of great misdemeanour Committed by Edward Starbuck of Dover with profession of Anabaptism for which he is to be proceeded against at the next Court of Assistants if evidence can be prepared by that time & it being very far for witnesses to travel to Boston at that season of the year. It is therefore ordered by this Court that the Secretary shall give Commission to Capt. Thomas Wiggan & Mr Edw. Smyth to send far such persons as they shall have notice of which are able to testify in the said cause & to take their testimony upon oath & certify the same to the secretary as soon as may be therein, if the cause shall so require.

Several families chose to relocate to Nantucket for the same reasons and this contemporary account clearly states the underlying reason for the exodus.

> THOMAS AND SARAH MACY *and their five children arrived in the fall of 1659. Incidentally, J, Thomas Mayhew, Sr. and Thomas Macy were cousins.*
>
> *Accompanying the Macys from Salisbury [Essex County] in Massachusetts Bay Colony were Edward Starbuck, Isaac Coleman, an orphan aged twelve years, and James Coffin, aged eighteen years.*
>
> *These were the pioneer settlers. Nothing is known of that historic voyage except that they stopped at Great Harbor (Edgartown) for comfort and further direction, and to take on one Dagget to pilot them on their voyage to (Maticat) Madaket.*
>
> *Macy was determined to relocate his homeland and to separate from his Salisbury associates and the tyranny of Puritan dress, custom, and clergy.*

The circumstances underlying the emigrations to Nantucket are described in the muse by G. H. Foulger:

> *Our Pilgrim fathers forth were driven By persecution's rod.*
> *And sought this isle among the waves.*
> *Where they could worship God.*
>
> *When Autumn's clouds lowered in the sky,*
> *Old Thomas dared the sea,*
> *With Edward nobly by his side,*
> *They'd die or they'd be free.*

Nantucket Odyssey, 1965

Another contemporary account of this voyage reads:

> *The early Anabaptists were promoters of a Free Church and freedom of religion independent of the state, along with the Quakers they were against war.*
>
> *It is not to be wondered at that Edward Starbuck was quite ready to leave Dover, despite his advanced age, and his interest in and around the town.*
>
> *He was fifty-five years of age when he joined Thomas Macy in his voyage from Salisbury to Nantucket. They arrived at Nantucket in the autumn of 1659, and remained during the winter at the outskirts of the island, removing later to a more central location, now called Cambridge.*
>
> *In the spring of 1660, Edward Starbuck returned to Dover for his family, all of whom returned with him except his daughters, Sarah Austin and Abigail Coffin. On his return to Nantucket he at once became active in official affairs, and was at one time magistrate. He died in Nantucket, February 4th 1690.*
>
> *He married Catherine Reynolds, a woman of Welsh parentage. Children, most of whom were born in England. One Sarah, married three times in Dover, New Hampshire.*

Proceeding their arrival in 1641 to Nantucket, William, Earl of Stirling sold his interest of the island to Thomas Mayhew.

Subsequently, in 1659, Mayhew sold nine-tenths of these shares to new arrivals on the island.

The original purchasers included Thomas Macy and his partner Edward Starbuck who paid thirty pounds for their share.

Further shares offered for sale were later intended to attract tradesmen skilled in weaving, milling, building and other trades. The settlement began to develop rapidly from 1659.

Shipping began to arrive but the original harbour silted up forcing the settlers to dismantle their houses and relocate about two miles to the northeast – Nantucket's present location.

As the settlement grew a further division of land occurred in 1678 after late arrivals protested at being second class citizens.

In 1835, Obed Macy wrote an account of an incident involving a whale in the pre-1672 colony.

He recounts how a whale entered the harbour and was pursued and killed by the settlers. The whale was described as a 'scragg', most likely a grey whale, a species that was hunted by early New England whalers.

This event reportedly triggered the birth of an industrial-scale whaling industry in Nantucket that extended to the open seas in a fleet of fully rigged whaling ships.

The schooner was the smallest of the whaling ships, usually with two masts and four sails and carrying two or three smaller whaleboats.

These smaller boats would be rowed by teams of men. A harpoon attached to a heavy rope would be thrown into a whale. When the whale was killed it would then be towed to the whale schooner and tied alongside, ready to be carried back to Nantucket's island shores.

With most employed in the Atlantic Ocean whaling schooners generally undertook six month voyages.

The importance of trade links with Britain influenced Nantucketer's decision to remain neutral at the outbreak of the American Revolution. This decision had ramifications for the island community after the Declaration of Independence following the defeat of the British.

The principal product of the whaling industry was whale oil, with premium quality taken from the head of the sperm whale.

It is believed that said oil is used as a means of adjusting the sperm whale's buoyancy, as the density of the spermaceti changes with heat, either externally of internally.

Used in the highest quality candles and known as the 'spermaceti candle', cheaper alternatives of the day were candles made from tallow.

There were several problems with tallow candles. The animal fat used to make the candle gave off a terrible odour when it burned, causing a house or office to fill with smoke. Tallow also melted quickly and in order to keep tallow candles burning wicks needed to be trimmed constantly.

Probably the biggest draw back in using tallow candles opposed to one produced from a sperm whale's oil was that it gave off a much lower light intensity level.

When in office as president of the United States of America, George Washington favoured the spermaceti candle for its superior quality of light.

CHAPTER 6

THE NANTUCKET STARBUCKS AND THE BIRTH OF WHALING

The island of Nantucket is colloquially known as 'The Little Grey Lady of the Sea'.

The name 'Nantucket' derives from the island's indigenous inhabitants the Wampanoag tribe.

As was his style, Edward became a prominent citizen of Nantucket and it is recorded he was Representative in the General Court and also an elder in the church.

His influence with North America's indigenous population was so effective that he was often called upon by townspeople to mediate in matters of potential conflict.

Edward was so respected by Massachusetts' indigenous people that the sachems (chiefs) gave him a deed for Coatue land, a pristine environment that sheltered Nantucket Harbour. This they bequeathed as a 'free and voluntary' gift, showing how Edward Starbuck was by all accounts a man of commanding presence.

Edward's social conduct and manners are in total contrast to that of other English settlers from *The Mayflower*.

Whereas Edward practised kindness and respect to America's original landlords, other settlers gave little in way of reverence or compassion to all met with.

An interesting fact is that while Edward had a harmonious relationship with the Wampanoag tribe, the Wampanoag were amongst those at war with the settlers of New England.

The attraction of the whaling industry of the 17th and 18th century was its products. Those who succeeded became the mega-rich of their era; similar to modern day equivalents of middle-eastern oil sheiks.

The attraction to their country was its contributing effect on the national GDP income.

What we know is that Edward Starbuck and his family were instrumental in the founding of the whaling industry based in Nantucket.

This was part of a wider whaling industry stretching along the coast of North America and so making it one of the largest whaling operations in the world.

Other large operations were located in Nova Scotia and its surrounding area.

Brest in Northern France and Milford Haven in South Wales are also mentioned as important areas, but a lack of railway connections limited the development of their harbours.

CHAPTER 7

THE QUAKER CONNECTION

Another link was discovered during our research when my wife Heather commented on the Quaker meeting house she recalled in the village of Pontrobert where she grew up in the 1950's – Pontrobert is a small village in Wales, twenty-four miles from where we live in Oswestry, England, which in turn is three miles from the Welsh border.

Built in the early 1700's, the meeting house still stands today and serves as an active meeting place for modern day Friends. Reportedly Willian Penn, the founder of the state of Pennsylvania visited this meeting house during his formative years within the Quaker movement. Penn travelled Europe inviting Anabaptists to his new American colony. Edward Starbuck became an Anabaptist at some stage in his life, it is not clear when that occurred as by the time of his rise to prominence in the new American settlements he was known as a religious man.

The Quakers and their likeminded Anabaptist cousins were a significant presence in the New World, due to their harsh treatment at the hands of the Protestants and Cavaliers in England and Europe during the 1600's. Yet, the New England Puritans where just as hostile to the Quakers and even banished some of the Quakers to the Caribbean.

Quaker and Anabaptist families including Edward Starbuck's decamped to Nantucket Island. There they prospered and founded the financially successful whaling industry of the 17th and early 18th century.

Holding a significant influence on America's early settlers William Penn was an English writer and religious thinker belonging to the Quakers (the Society of Friends), a sect of religious radicals reviled by respectable society.

Penn was the son of a wealthy and successful Admiral of the Royal Navy who had been rewarded for his military service by the granting of substantial lands in Ireland. In later years, King Charles II transferred ownership of great tracts of land in North America as settlement of debts owed by the crown to the Penn estate.

On inheriting this wealth from his family, Penn departed for the Americas in 1770 to stake his claim and founded the City of Philadelphia, around which the state of Pennsylvania was eventually formed.

Philadelphia quickly became a cornerstone of the New World infrastructure for many reasons, not least of which was its geographical location.

The state of Philadelphia subsequently made a historic contribution to the world and the development of freedom. It was in this endevour that Benjamin Franklin was deeply involved.

As an intellectual centre and business hub, Philadelphia attracted the most prominent people of the time. In 1723, Benjamin Franklin was among them.

Philadelphia at the time was the largest English speaking city in the world outside of London, and so described as *'one of the new wonders of the world'* and *'America's first town'*.

Although Franklin disliked the 'stiff rumped' Quakers, he devoted himself to the principles of unity - setting foundations for the revolutionary army that was to oppose English rule in the revolutionary war of 1790.

Philadelphia became a truly cosmopolitan city and was described by John Adams as *'a place where 13 clocks could be made to strike as one'*.

CHAPTER 8

'THE THREE BROTHERS'

With other prominent families the Starbuck's developed their whaling industry in Nantucket, beginning at the latter part of the 17th century with wooden sailing ships fishing the Atlantic.

As the industry prospered and expanded cruises of several months were required to hunt for more whales.

Once again the sperm whale was the most prized because of its superior oil obtained from sperm whales, a translucent yellowish waxy liquid that holds a very faint scent of raw milk.

A different composition from common whale oil obtained from condensed blubber, sperm whale oil derives from the whale's large head that contains a wide cavity called the spermaceti organ. This cavity is filled with three to four tons of oil (spermaceti oil) and consists of a mixture of triglycerides and waxes.

Although traditionally called an 'oil', it is technically a liquid wax. Not only utilised for candles favoured by presidents, sperm whale oil has been used among other things as an ingredient in soap, explosives, and even margarine.

Sperm whale oil was seen as being extremely valuable due to its unique properties. Being able to withstand high temperatures led it to being used as a lubricant in fast-moving machinery of the day.

Whalers knew that a sperm whale's mysterious oil could fetch a much higher price than regular oil due to its smokeless and odourless burn.

Determined to capture a sperm whale's plentiful bounty whale hunts were soon extended to last for more than one year.

These expeditions would take a whale's pursuers out into the Pacific Ocean via the perilous seawaters of Cape Horn, a rocky headland on the Hornos Island in Southern Chile's Tierra del Fuego archipelago.

Yet as the industry became more complex not all its leaders went to sea.

Joseph Starbuck

Joseph Starbuck (1774–1861) worked best on the books and the day-to-day management of his father's business. He particularly excelled in the planning and execution of the business' schedules

His father Thomas was initially surprised his son displayed no desire to go to sea. But as Joseph matured he realised his son's considerable talents were best utilised on shore.

Joseph married Sally Gardner in 1797 and had ten children, three of whom died at a young age, but three brothers, Matthew, George and William survived.

While Joseph's brothers went to sea hunting whale as masters of their ships, Joseph concentrated on the shore operation concerned with turning whale oil into industrial products. His business thrived.

In 1807, Joseph and Sally built the house of their dreams out of brick. What is significant about brick is in its location. Nantucket holds no brick clay in its geology, meaning all bricks have to be imported, so advertising an owner's wealth.

Other 'founding families' such as the Foulgers and the Coffins had built imposing brick houses in Main Street, the most prominent location in the town.

Joseph brought his sons into his business under the name Joseph Starbuck and Sons. About this time he contracted for a new whale ship to be built in Old Rochester. He named the ship *The Three Brothers*.

In his book titled *Three Bricks and Three Brothers – The Story of the Nantucket Whale Oil Merchant Joseph Starbuck*, Will Gardner writes:

> "*Joseph sat in the sun while the ship came in… he could see Matthew and George in their trim clothes and tall hats standing at the end of the wharf where the ship would tie up.*
>
> *William was there with them. The hum of the talk, the whistles and calls, the slow moving ship with her fluttering flags – and in the foreground on the wharf the black greasy casks of oil, all stirred him deeply.*
>
> *This was Starbuck success. The blue-and-white barred flags said more to him than anyone knew.*"

Joseph died on 9th March 1861 with his whole family by his bedside, including Matthew, George and William. His last whispered words were distinctly heard to be *"three brothers"*.

Even after Joseph's death the family were still progressing their business technically.

The following was written about the whaler, *Tillie E. Starbuck*.

> "This vessel was the first full-rigged ship ever built of iron in the United States. She was launched on April 14, 1883.

The Tillie E. Starbuck was owned until the end of the nineties by W. H. Starbuck. She could not, however, compare as regards speed with many of the wooden ships of her size and date.

After being owned by Luckenbach for a year or two at the beginning of the twentieth century, the Tillie E. Starbuck came under the control of Welch Co. of San Francisco.

In 1905 she got badly ashore and had to have a number of new plates put into her bottom by the Union Iron Works at San Francisco.

The Tillie E. Starbuck was lost off the Horn whilst bound out to Honolulu from New York in 1907."

CHAPTER 9

THE DECLINE OF WHALING IN NANTUCKET

The whaling industry of Nantucket was in sharp decline by 1850.

Along with the silting up of the harbour a devastating fire swept through Nantucket on 13th July 1846.

When William M. Geary closed his hat shop for the day on Main Street, Nantucket on Monday, 13th July 1846, he walked home unaware that his shop's fireplace used to warm hat making irons had a blocked stovepipe.

Spotted by the watchman of the town's South Tower the fire started around 11pm. With up to ten firefighting companies on the island their efforts to extinguish the fast growing fire were unsuccessful. Nantucket would see forty acres of its buildings reduced to ash that night.

On the 8th February, 1847 a report was submitted to the town by an appointed investigation committee. The committee included William C. Starbuck.

The committee deduced that due to no single leadership and differing opinions within the island's firefighting companies a weak response to raging fires was produced. It was also said that with little rain in the days leading up to the fire Nantucket's downtown area of predominantly wooden building were dry to the bone.

The committee therefore concluded that Nantucket's narrow streets and the evening's brisk sea winds made for perfect conditions for a fire to spread quickly through the town from William M. Geary's hat shop's blocked stovepipe.

Nantucket Town's devastating fire would see to driving away a large number of its inhabitants.

In result New Bedford became the new centre of the whaling industry, benefitting from both a deep-water port and a railroad connection necessary for the transportation of whale oil.

The final blow to Nantucket came during the American Civil War when the Confederate Navy sank many of the whaling vessels.

The importance of whale oil as fuel for oil lamps was eclipsed by the discovery of kerosene by Abraham Gesner (1797-1864). The discovery of the Drake Well in Pennsylvania in 1859 opened up a vast industry for oil wells and a plentiful supply of cheap kerosene.

When visiting the Henry Ford Museum in Detroit, Heather and I attended an exhibition displaying the transition of lamp fuel from whale oil to kerosene, as used in the Ford offices.

The economic importance of the whaling industry era is now likened to the modern mineral oil industry.

The established prosperity of this industry was later severely affected by Edward Drake's invention of the oil-drilling rig in Titusville, Pennsylvania in 1859.

This facilitated a cost-effective extraction and consequently more competitively priced petroleum, which is easily and cheaply converted to kerosene, particularly for use in lighting lamps, thus replacing oil made from whales.

Nantucket Island was left isolated until the mid-1950's when property developers bought up large sections of the island to create up-market residences for the wealthy.

Nantucket is now one of the wealthiest counties in the United States.

CHAPTER 10

THE MILFORD HAVEN STARBUCKS

Founded in 1793 by Sir William Hamilton, who initially invited Quaker whalers from Nantucket to live in his town, Milford Haven in South Wales has a long association with the sea.

A town and community in Pembrokeshire, Wales, its Welsh name Aberdaugleddau, means *'mouth of the two Rivers Cleddau'*. To the north side of the Milford Haven Waterway an estuary forms a natural harbour, one that has been used as a port since the Middle Ages.

In 1797 the Navy Board established a dock in Milford Haven where seven ships were built including HMS Milford.

In 1802, Nelson was invited to visit Milford Haven's new dock as part of his grand tour. He was accompanied on his visit by Sir William Hamilton and his wife Lady Emma Hamilton. An interesting trio as Nelson and Lady Hamilton were lovers.

Nelson gave a speech in the New Inn, a new building in the aptly named Hamilton terrace. The inn was renamed the Admiral Lord Nelson Hotel in honour of the distinguished sailor.

Sir William presented the hotel with a portrait of Nelson by the Italian artist Leonardo Guzzardi; it was subsequently relocated to Admiralty House in London.

The portrait is in stark contrast to the idealised portraits often produced of the victor of Trafalgar. It is perhaps more lifelike in showing the scars and strain of long years at sea from a young age.

The scar above Nelson's right eye resulted from cannon-shot shrapnel during land action in Corsica in 1793. He eventually lost the sight in that eye, possibly from a detached retina. By this time he is also missing his right arm, lost in an engagement at Santa Cruz in 1797.

Many of Milford Haven's streets are named after those prominent in the town's history.

Starbuck Road is named after one of the Quaker whaling families from America who were brought to Milford Haven by Charles Francis Greville, nephew of landowner Sir William Hamilton, who had plans to develop the town of Milford Haven in the late 18th century.

Greville had decided to create a whaling industry in Milford Haven and began negotiating with the whalers of Nantucket to relocate themselves to South Wales.

The town and port of Nantucket was at that time the centre of the American whaling industry.

Quaker families had originally formed the backbone of this industry, but through declaring their neutrality in war, their business prospects were adversely affected by the outcome of the War of Independence. When the fighting ended in 1783 with victory for the colonialists, many Nantucket families began to look for new opportunities elsewhere.

Three Nantucket families agreed to go to Milford Haven: the Foulgers, the Rotch family, and their cousins the Starbucks. They presented Greville with a list of requirements for suitable docks and quays to be constructed, including land for a Quaker meeting house, burial ground and housing.

Some arrived in Milford Haven in 1792 but it took until the end of the decade for the Rotch family to join, at which time the building of the town has begun following the 1790 Act of Parliament.

The street plan adopted the American grid system and many of the fine buildings erected at this time still remain.

The architectural style of Milford Haven's buildings echoed the style of those built in New England, with the grey, shingle-clad houses described by contemporaries as:

> *"substantial, if somewhat austere, staring boldly out to sea, in keeping with the style and location of their original houses."*

Daniel and Samuel Starbuck Jr built their houses on either side of what was Front Street (now Dartmouth Street, named after their last homeport).

Of the Rotch family, Benjamin Rotch only stayed for a short while before moving to Dunkirk to manage his father's business there.

However, following the outbreak of war between France and England, he and his family escaped to London, with Benjamin Rotch escaping in a flour barrel. He would later become the Whig MP for Knaresborough after entering Parliament in 1831.

The Starbucks and the Foulgers also left Milford Haven and embarked for Dartmouth, Nova Scotia, Canada. Located on the eastern shore of Halifax Harbour, Dartmouth has the nickname of *City of Lakes*, so called after the large number of lakes located within its boundaries.

The result of those of vast whaling knowledge leaving Milford Haven, namely the Starbuck, Foulger and Rotch families, was that Milford Haven never became a whaling centre.

Yet past memories of American whaling communities remain to this day within Milford Haven.

Built in Hamilton Terrace in 1797, the home of the then surgeon to the whaling fleet is now the Belhaven House Hotel, and other street names recall more whaling families such as the Bunkers.

The Quaker-built Friends Meeting House in Priory Road was built in 1811.

Quakers have often felt called to *'live adventurously'* and have documented in tapestry the families including the Starbucks and Foulgers who opted to sail three thousand miles eastwards to Milford Haven.

This period of the town's history is captured by the *'Milford Friends'* panel in the Quaker Tapestry project, which was completed in 1996.

As a further indication of Cape Cod's influence on the Milford Haven's history, there is a restaurant in the town called *Martha's Vineyard*.

CHAPTER 11

BENJAMIN FRANKLIN AND NANTUCKET ISLAND

Benjamin Franklin's mother's side were the Foulgers, who as noted were also one of the founding families of Nantucket. In 1720 her daughter Anna Foulger married into another founding family, that of William Starbuck.

It is impossible to mention Benjamin Franklin without giving a summary of his achievements in life.

Born 17th January 1706 in Boston, Massachusetts, his father Josiah Franklin, was married twice with Benjamin being the youngest son of seventeen children. His father's occupation was as a soap and tallow candle maker.

Leaving school at the age of ten his career got off to an inconspicuous start. It was impossible to anticipate his life achievements in their output and range.

Described as a renowned scientist, inventor and polymath he was also a writer, diplomat, printer and publisher and a highly regarded political philosopher.

Franklin became one of the founders of the United States of America and sits with George Washington. He is the epitome of a self-made man through self-education. His description as a leading author, political theorist, politician and postmaster only scratches the surface of his contributions.

At the age of twelve he and his brother began a career in printing. A fall out with his brother resulted in Franklin leaving for New York and to Philadelphia where he found more work as a printer. To balance his limited budget he reverted to vegetarianism, contending that it gave him more energy, saved on the effort of eating meat and that vegetables required less digestive energy.

At the age of eighteen he was induced to go to London for an exciting commission which did not exist. While working as a compositor he was offered work in Philadelphia. Franklin soon became a successful newspaper editor in Philadelphia, and at the age of twenty-three he published the Pennsylvania Gazette, a leading publication within the eyes of the colonists.

Consequently, his career progressed and he set up his own printing house. In 1732 he produced his famous Port Richard Almanac, which was described as only second in popularity to the Bible.

Appointed postmaster of Philadelphia by the British Crown in 1737, Franklin had a long and distinguished career in this service, eventually serving as joint postmaster general for the British colonies from 1753 until being dismissed in 1774. This was due to reasons of being too sympathetic to the American revolutionary cause.

In spite of the demands of his business he still found time for public affairs including founding the 'American Philosophical Society' which developed into the University of Pennsylvania.

Understanding the potential of the postal service he was one of the founders of 'mail order' in 1744 when he was first to provide a library book loan service where borrowers could borrow books which were too expensive for individuals to purchase.

With so many interests outside his business, at the age of forty-two he sold it in 1748. Comfortable wealth gave him freedom to pursue his other interests.

His role as an Assembly member, politician and diplomat included developing relations with England and her colonies, and eventually with France where he was received with honour.

In 1757 he moved to London and rented a house at 36 Craven Street between Charing Cross Station and Trafalgar Square. He stayed there until 1775. While there he continued with his American political and diplomatic work.

In 2006 it was restored as the Benjamin Franklin Museum and became the world's only remaining Franklin home where he once lived.

His scientific work received recognition with a range of awards including honorary doctorates from The University of St. Andrews in 1759 and from Oxford University in 1762. This resulted in him sometimes being addressed as Dr Franklin. There was also recognition from Franklin's network of learned scientists, inventors and consequential societies. One such society was the Lunar Society which he records he corresponded with and visited.

The Lunar Society was a group of like-minded people who were interested in new discoveries, so called because they travelled to meet as a group on full-moon nights when moonlight gave enough illumination for them to travel by horseback.

In July 2017 I visited London and the museum of the Benjamin Franklin House, There I met with Mallory Horrill - front of house and marketing manager, who kindly furthered my exploration.

Although Franklin never ran for president he was the first United States ambassador to France and Sweden, and in 1787 helped found the Society for Political Inquiries, a society dedicated to improving knowledge of government.

Benjamin Franklin also played a vital role as one of America's eight *Founding Fathers*, and went on to draft the Declaration of Independence and the U.S. Constitution.

Of all eight founding fathers Franklin held a unique contribution, that of being the only one to have signed four of the key documents that went on to establish the United States of America.

These documents were:

The Declaration of Independence – 4th July, 1776
The Treaty of Alliance with France – 6th February, 1778
The Treaty of Paris – 3rd September, 1783
The U.S. Constitution – 17th September, 1787

Of all of Benjamin Franklin's achievements, he is celebrated for his experiments with electricity.

In the mid-18th century electricity was seen as mere entertainment were magic tricks produced sparks and shocks. To scientists of the day electricity was of little use to the world.

Franklin's interest in electricity suited his inquisitive mind. It would be in his natural curiosity for the world that he would arrive to an important notion.

His ideas were focused on electricity, but more so lightning. Franklin had observed similarities between the two. Both produced light, and both exploded with a loud crashing noise. These observations led Franklin to deduce that electricity and lightning were the same thing.

Writing letters to fellow scientists in London, Franklin's colleague's felt his words held valuable information and in 1751 saw to publishing his letters in a small book titled *Experiments and Observations on Electricity*.

One of Franklin's letters set out a strategy to prove that electricity and lightning were the same. For his plan to work he needed a steep hill or a tall building. At the time

Philadelphia had neither. Franklin soon formulated a solution involving a kite and a key.

Needing to get close enough to the clouds to attract lightning, on a stormy summer's evening in 1752, and with the assistance of his son William, Franklin made a simple kite from a large silk handkerchief and attached a metal wire to its top to attract the lightning. He then attached a wet hemp string which would rapidly conduct an electrical charge. To the string he attached a metal key and then with his son's help raised the kite aloft into the storm clouds.

Franklin's kite was not struck by lightning as popular myth often tells; this would only have resulted in Franklin and his son being electrocuted. The kite instead picked up the storm's ambient electrical charge.

Moving his finger near the key, the key's negative charges were attracted to his hand and a spark was produced. Franklin then touched his knuckle to the key where he received a significant electric shock.

Franklin's experiment demonstrated the connection between lightning and electricity and that electricity could be harnessed and so be utilised.

From his experiment of kite and key came the invention of the lightning rod; mounted on the top of a tall building, a metal rod runs down its side and earths into the ground, so protecting the structure from lightning strikes.

Franklin's inventions did not stop at lightning rods. In later years as his eyesight began to fail he invented eyeglasses with two distinct optical powers, these are now known as bifocal lenses, and with homes in colonial America heated by fireplaces, Franklin invented the *Franklin Stove* in 1742. A metal-lined fireplace positioned in the middle of a room, its rear baffles improved airflow, used less wood and provided more heat and less smoke than an open fireplace.

The Robert H Smith Scholarship Centre

Robert H. Smith (1928 –2009) was an American building developer and philanthropist. A key supporter of Benjamin Franklin House, he was particularly passionate about the heritage and reach of American democracy.

To honour Robert H. Smith at the British Library in May 2010, the Benjamin Franklin House held the inaugural Robert H. Smith Annual Lecture in American Democracy.

A key scholarship centre initiative is the annual Benjamin Franklin House Symposium in association with the Eccles Centre for American Studies. It features leading speakers in fields such as science, politics and business, discussing issues inspired by Franklin's life and work.

The Papers of Benjamin Franklin' were established under the joint patronages of Yale University and the American Philosophical Society.

This involves the analysis and uploading of Franklin's written work online. The Friends of Franklin also help to sustain the enterprise.

Robert H. Smith's philanthropy focused on many other historic preservation efforts beside that of Benjamin Franklin's former London home.

In 2008, Smith donated close to half of the $15 million cost to renovate President Lincoln's Cottage, and as an avid collector of European paintings, he donated his collection to the National Gallery of Art in Washington D.C., America.

It was during his time serving as President of the gallery between 1993 and 2003 that the museum's works expanded considerably.

A German Connection

As Benjamin Franklin prepared to leave for America he was given recognition for his inventions by the Hanoverian Royal Society of Sciences in Lower Saxony, Germany, in the Kingdom of Hanover at Pyrmont now Bad Pyrmont.

During the Cold War of 1959-61, I was a conscripted National Service solider in the Royal Engineers.

I spent twenty months in Hamelin; the town made famous by Robert Browning's poem *'The Pied Piper of Hamelin'*. Bad Pyrmont is part of Hamelin-Pyrmont District, which I visited on several occasions. It is one of the most attractive towns to visit with its classical architecture.

Of recognition given by the Hanoverian Royal Society of Sciences Franklin writes:

> *"To-morrow I set out with my Friend Dr. Pringle [now Sir John] on a Journey to Pyrmont, where he goes to drink the Waters; but I hope more from the Air and Exercise."*
>
> *"I accordingly went to Pyrmont, where I drank the Waters some Days; but relying more on the Air and Exercise of Travelling, I proceeded to Hanover."* (1766)

After Franklin's visit to Bad Pyrmont he left for America and continued his work including partitioning and freeing the indigenous population from slavery in the Confederate South. He received further recognition including MScs from Harvard and Yale. Despite his mammoth work load he still had time to return to Nantucket.

What had become knowledge to him in his duties as Postmaster was that ships crossing the North Atlantic took two to three weeks longer than if sailing north of Boston.

He was aware the fishermen of Nantucket knew the reason - the ocean currents coming from the Caribbean past Nantucket were warmer than the surrounding seas and could be identified because whales avoided the warm water.

In 1769 – 1770 Franklin met his cousin Timothy Foulger. Together they plotted the current and produced a chart for the benefit of the sailors. The significant chart is the Gulf Stream which crosses the Atlantic and has an essential warming influence on the British Isles.

There is an abundance of research about Franklin including *The Autobiography of Benjamin Franklin* (Cassels National Library 1889). The book records Franklin's life and how he became one of the first to publish how he achieved his phenomenal output through self-management.

One of history's great managers of the self, Benjamin Franklin's attempts to arrive at greater virtue were unrelenting. To do this he kept a log.

> *"I ruled each page with red ink, so as to have seven columns, one for each day of the week, marking each column with a letter for the day.*
>
> *I crossed these columns with thirteen red lines, marking the beginning of each line with the first letter of one of the virtues, on which line, and in its proper column might mark, by a little black spot, every fault I found upon examination to have been committed respecting that virtue upon that day."*

Franklin defines such principles in his autobiography:

> *"I grew convinced that truth sincerity and integrity, in dealings between man and man, were of the upmost importance to the felicity of life… to practice them over while I lived".*

Franklin identified his thirteen virtues with precepts:

1. Temperance:
Eat not to dullness; drink not to elevation
2. Silence:
Speak not but what may benefit others or yourself; avoid trifling conversation.
3. Order:
Let all your things have their places; let each part of your business have its time.
4. Resolution:
Resolve to perform what you ought; perform without fail what you resolve.
5. Frugality:
Do good to others or yourself; that is, waste nothing.
6. Industry:
Lose no time; be always employed in something useful.
7. Sincerity:
Use no hurtful deceit; think innocently and justly; and, if you speak, speak accordingly.
8. Justice:
Wrong none by doing injuries, or omitting the benefits that are your duty.
9. Moderation:
Avoid extremes; forbear resenting in- juries, so much as you think they deserve.
10. Cleanliness:
Tolerate no uncleanliness in body, clothes, or habitation.
11. Tranquillity:
Be not disturbed at trifles or accidents unavoidable.
12. Chastity:
Adhere to the sanctity of chastity.
13. Humility:
Imitate Jesus and Socrates.

Franklin further wrote:

> *"My intention being to acquire the habitude of all these virtues, I judged it would be well not to distract my attention by attempting the whole at once, but to fix it on one of them at a time; and, when I should be master of that, then to proceed to another; and so on, till I should have gone through the thirteen."*

In his book *Moonwalking with Einstein* (2012) Joshua Foer identifies that one way to improve one's understanding of a topic is to replicate how an expert thinks their way through it. Foer identifies that Anders Ericson and his team describe Franklin's application in his autobiography.

Newt Gingrich, the recognised researcher and politician who was the US Speaker of the House of Representative 1995 – 1999 writes in his book *To Renew America* 1995.

> *"The convention heeded Franklin's eloquent plea and shortly after was able to resolve its differences and complete the Constitution of the United States."*

> *"For Ben Franklin, solving public problems mean starting volunteer fire departments, volunteer philosophical societies, and volunteer libraries. Franklin was postmaster general for the colonies and knew there were things that had to be done at a national level. But generally he turned neither to national government nor to state and local government but to organized volunteers to get things done."*

As an epitaph to the man who helped shape the world, one of his last conspicuous acts was to continue with his crusade against slavery.

As the owner of two slaves he reflected that it was wrong and began his actions by releasing them.

In 1784 the previous arguments for the freedom of slaves was reorganised as the *Pennsylvania Society for Promoting the Abolition of Slavery for the Relief of Free Negroes Unlawfully Held in Bondage.*

As a consequence, he wrote the following:

> *Petition from the Pennsylvania Society for the Abolition of Slavery to the Senate & House of Representatives of the United States.*
>
> "The Memorial of the Pennsylvania Society for promoting the Abolition of Slavery, the relief of free Negroes unlawfully held in bondage, & the Improvement of the Condition of the African Races."
> *Respectfully Sheweth,*
>
> *That from a regard for the happiness of Mankind an Association was formed several years since in this State by a number of her Citizens of various religious denominations for promoting the Abolition of Slavery & for the relief of those unlawfully held in bondage.*
>
> *A just & accurate Conception of the true Principles of liberty, as it spread through the land, produced accessions to their numbers, many friends to their Cause, & a legislative Co-operation with their views, which, by the blessing of Divine Providence, have been successfully directed to the relieving from bondage a large number of their fellow Creatures of the African Race.*
>
> *They have also the Satisfaction to observe, that in consequence of that Spirit of Philanthropy & genuine liberty which is generally diffusing its beneficial Influence, similar Institutions are gradually forming at home & abroad.*
>
> *"That mankind are all formed by the same Almighty being, alike objects of his care & equally designed for the enjoyment of happiness the Christian religion teaches us to believe & the Political Creed of America fully coincides with the position. Your*

Memorialists, particularly engaged in attending to the distresses arising from slavery, believe it their indispensable duty to present this subject to your notice.

They have observed with great satisfaction that many important & salutary powers are vested in you for 'promoting the welfare & securing the blessings of liberty to the People of the United States.' And as they conceive, that these blessings ought rightfully to be administered, without distinction of colour, to all descriptions of people, so they indulge themselves in the pleasing expectation, that nothing, which can be done for the relieve of the unhappy objects of their care, will be either omitted or delayed.

From a persuasion that equal liberty was originally the Portion, It is still the Birth right of all men, & influenced by the strong ties of Humanity & the Principles of their Institution, your Memorialists conceive themselves bound to use all justifiable endeavours to loosen the bounds of Slavery and promote a general Enjoyment of the blessings of Freedom.

Under these Impressions they earnestly entreat your serious attention to the Subject of Slavery, that you will be pleased to countenance the Restoration of liberty to those unhappy Men, who alone, in this land of Freedom, are degraded into perpetual Bondage, and who, amidst the general Joy of surrounding Freemen, are groaning in Servile Subjection, that you will devise means for removing this Inconsistency from the Character of the American People, that you will promote mercy and Justice towards this distressed Race, & that you will Step to the very verge of the Powers vested in you for discouraging every Species of Traffick in the Persons of our fellow men."

Philadelphia 3rd February 1790
Benjamin Franklin, President of the Society

This must have been one of his last acts as Franklin died 17th April 1790.

CHAPTER 12

HOW COFFEE CAME OUT OF NANTUCKET

Folgers

After the great fire that destroyed much of Nantucket in 1846, many of the residents left the island to seek their fortunes elsewhere. This was the era of the Californian Gold Rush.

Beginning on the 24th January 1848, after James W. Marshall found gold at Sutter's Mill in Coloma, California, the Gold Rush became the largest mass migration in U.S. history. News of Marshall finding gold brought an estimated 300,000 people to California from the rest of the United States and abroad.

With hopes set on the riches gold promised a fifteen-year-old James Folger and two of his brothers left Nantucket and travelled across the country to San Francisco in 1850.

On arriving to California James' two brothers left for the mines while James started work for William H. Bovee, founder of Pioneer Steam Coffee & Spice Mills.

Part of the progress for the company in its earlier stages was improvements to its customer service. At this stage Californians had to buy green coffee beans and roast and grind them for use.

This proved to be a laborious chore and often put potential buyers off purchasing from the Pioneer Steam Coffee & Spice Mills.

With the help of Folger as a carpenter, Bovee built a factory to process the beans for the customers for immediate use.

They also chartered redundant Nantucket whale boats to bring coffee from South America to San Francisco.

Folger progressed with the company which prospered until the economy collapsed following the American Civil War. He then refinanced the company, bought out his fellow partners in 1872 and renamed it J.A. Folger & Co - (Folger's Coffee).

In 1889 James Folger died and was succeeded as CEO by his twenty-six year old eldest son James A. Folger II.

Under his management in the 1900's the company grew exponentially. This was primarily down to salesman Frank P. Atha.

Chiefly selling coffee in the Californian area, Atha suggested to James Folger II that he open and manage a Folgers Coffee plant in Texas.

The company developed dramatically after Atha opened the Texas plant.

The Folger brand became one of the leaders in the North American coffee market and the largest in the world.

Selling ground, instant, and single-use pod coffee produced in the United States, Folgers coffee has also become a popular brand globally.

The company was acquired by Procter & Gamble in 1963 and since 2008 continues now as a subsidiary of John Smucker & Company.

Starbucks

The first Starbucks coffee shop was opened in 1971.

Founded by three partners in Seattle who had met while students at the University of San Francisco, they were Jerry Baldwin, an English teacher, Zen Siegl, a history teacher and Gordon Bowker, a writer.

Their origin had been a small outlet named Peat's Coffee & Tea in 1966. Reflecting on their start-up they identified that Seattle lacked a quality coffee shop that produced quality aromatic coffee.

Setting an objective of providing high quality coffee they searched for a brand name for their product.

Searching for a dramatic, adventurous and memorable brand name they looked to American author Herman Melville's 1851 novel *Moby Dick, or The Whale*. This was in view of linking coffee to the adventurous spirit of Nantucket Island's seafaring whaling community.

Melville's book is a travel-log adventure about the life of whalers and their prey based upon Melville's time at sea, the draw of which he found magnetic.

Melville had visited Nantucket. Meeting the town's local community, including the Starbuck family, he also met Owen Chase who had written a log which was a narrative of the wreck of the whaleship The Essex. Chase was first mate on The Essex which sailed from Nantucket with George Pollard as her captain.

Chase's log is re-issued in the 2000 novel *In the Heart of the Sea* by Nathaniel Philbrick.

Well into their voyage in the Equatorial Pacific, The Essex met with a tragic accident and a set of unique and unpredictable events. While the three harpooning boats were whale hunting, a bull sperm whale rammed the side of the wooden Essex causing it to list. Attacking the stern of the ship The Essex began to sink.

The harpooning crews returned to the ship which had to be abandoned. Collecting what provisions they could the ship's crew set sail for land in three boats.

Not precisely sure of their position as sea charts were still being developed, it was determined they were as far from civilised settlements as was possible.

Log records show the boats got separated. As each ran out of water and food the survivors ate the bodies of their dead crew mates. As survival became more critical the survivors drew lots as to who would be killed before committing acts of cannibalism.

Eventually the three boats were rescued and eight of the twenty crew were saved and returned home.

Inspired by Chase's story of The Essex, his time on Nantucket Island and those met with, Melville began to write his literary classic.

In *Moby Dick,* Melville tells of the ship Pequod. Sailing from Nantucket, The Pequod is captained by Ahab and his first mate Starbuck. Where Captain Ahab is driven by pure emotion, it is Starbuck who provides the voice of reason aboard ship.

On a previous whaling expedition Ahab had been attacked by an albino whale, so named Moby Dick. All but dying, Ahab lost a leg and an arm in the incident.

The purpose for Ahab's voyage was to find and kill the whale Moby Dick in an obsessive quest for revenge.

After reading and thoroughly searching through Moby Dick the original partners of a soon to be named Starbucks considered using a name from one of the Pequod's crew. After much deliberation they agreed it did not have the right ring to it.

Returning to Melville's book they looked to Ahab's first mate Starbuck, a character named after those Melville had met with when visiting Nantucket's island community.

All partners agreed unanimously that the name Starbuck held the right connotations searched for.

With the partners having discovered the name the business was promoted and so progressed.

Having established Starbucks coffee brand it attracted the attention of Howard Schultz, Chairman and CEO of Starbucks, who tells his story in his book *'Pour Your Heart Into It: How Starbucks Built A Company One Cup At A Time'* (1997)- co-authored by Dori Jones Yang.

It is his personal record beginning with how he was born into a Jewish family ambitious for their children as they grew up in in 1950's Brooklyn, New York.

Driven by what he describes as a culture of 'fear of failure' he learnt to be competitive and became a good athlete and a supporter of traditional American sport.

Being the first member of his family to go to a college he went on to obtain a BA from North Michigan University. Applying his education, his career developed as he secured well-paying prestigious jobs involving travel in America.

It would be on a trip to Seattle where he would meet the Starbucks team who he himself described as a small chain with just five coffee houses.

On seeing the theory behind Starbucks and how popular each of the five coffee houses were, Schultz was immediately attracted to its novel concept.

A concept which saw the utilising of high-grade ingredients served within a customer sensitive background.

Returning home he reflected on what he had seen:

> *"For my part I saw Starbucks not for what it was, but for what it could be. It had immediately captivated me with its combination of passion and authenticity.*
>
> *If it could expand nationwide, romancing the Italian artistry of espresso-making as well as offering fresh roasted coffee beans, I gradually realized it could reinvent as age-old commodity and appeal to millions of people as strongly as it appealed to me."*

Much to the surprise of his family he negotiated to join the original founders in 1982. By 1987 Schultz had become CEO of Starbucks which grew as a company into one of the world's most recognised brands.

In the Harvard Business Review, March-April, 2000, innovation experts Vijay Vishwanath and David Harding of Bain & Co Boston Office Works describe *'The Starbuck Effect'*, telling how Starbucks' approach transformed the American coffee market by making coffee a consumer product. It notes that:

> *"Ten years ago only 3% of all coffee sold in the United States was priced at a premium – at least 25% higher than value brands. Today 40% of coffee is sold at premium prices".*

Not only do Starbucks continually improve the quality and range of its products, they are also sensitive to individual customers and their instore environment.

Howard Schultz is described as *'the Bill Gates of coffee'*. He was succeeded as CEO in 2017 by Kevin Johnson.

Reflecting on his success he quotes:

> *"Whenever you see a successful business, someone once made a courageous decision."*   Peter F. Drucker

CHAPTER 13

CONCLUSIONS

This odyssey of discovery has taken just over 20 years, with the Starbuck name drawing together three main threads: the seafaring Norsemen or Vikings, the whaling industry of Nantucket, and the establishment of the coffee industry in America.

It is not surprising that with his Viking genes Edward Starbuck undertook the hazardous crossing to America in the early 1600's to seek his fortune in the New World.

What is perhaps more poignant is that he gave up everything for a second time in defence of his staunch religious beliefs. What is clear is that he had both the courage of his convictions and the entrepreneurial drive to relocate his family yet again from Dover to Nantucket.

A testament to Edward Starbuck's personal qualities is the fact that he rapidly became a man of substance, earning the respect of his peers in Nantucket.

The growth and success of the whaling industry would have been dependent upon highly developed maritime skills as established by the Vikings. When the opportunity presented itself the Starbucks again crossed the Atlantic in an entrepreneurial spirit to attempt the establishment of a whaling industry in South Wales, subsequently journeying back to America when this failed to materialise.

Included has been the account of Benjamin Franklin's association with Nantucket through the inter-marrying between the Foulger and Starbuck families. He is regarded as one of the great men of history and as one of the founding fathers of America. It is interesting that he continued his connection with his cousin in Nantucket to chart the Gulf Stream.

The third element of this study is the connection to the coffee industry both past and present, but starting in the mid-1800's and coinciding with the decline of the whaling industry.

Some of the Foulger family related to Benjamin Franklin sought new fortunes on the mainland and eventually became very successful traders in coffee while some of the Starbucks had a lesser role.

An interesting part of the story is when the whaling industry declined they focused on their explorer skills and moved forward. This move was as entrepreneurs into one of the next growth industries in America, that of coffee.

Of the history of the Foulgers we only have outline information at present.

What is shown is that John Foulger was born circa 1590 or 1592/3 in Norwich, Norfolk, the son of a father of the same name, his mother being Elizabeth.

John Jnr. is recorded as migrating to New England during the Puritan Great Migration of 1620 to 1640. Some reports record that he was married by 1615/16 in Norwich to Meribeh Gibbs.

In another report he left for New England as a widower and married her on his arrival. - also, that John died in Nantucket circa 1660 and that his widow now named Meribell was alive in 1664. What is established is that he was accompanied by his son Peter who was about eighteen years old at the time.

There is no evidence that his DNA has been determined and traced. What is clear is that John is described as Benjamin Franklin's great grandfather.

Appendix i

The University of Leicester's 'What's in a Name?'

Seeking Viking descendants in the north of England

Part of the project: 'What's in a name?'
Funded by the Wellcome Trust

Researchers: Prof Mark Jobling & Dr. Turi King

University Road
Leicester LE1 7RH · UK
Tel: 0116 252 3377
Mobile: 07512 586 493
Email: surnames@le.ac.uk
web: www.le.ac.uk/genetics/maj4

Dear Participant,

Thank you for expressing interest in participating in our study of genetics and the history of the people of Britain.

In this study we aim to look at the proportion of Viking ancestry in different parts of the north of England. The only criterion for participating is that you are a man whose father's father was born in the county of Cumbria, Lancashire, Cheshire, Yorkshire, Durham or Northumberland. Simply brushing the inside of your cheek provides us with the sample we need, and full instructions are enclosed.

We are carrying out this work as a research project and thus it is absolutely free for you to take part. In return, we will provide you with a summary of the results, designed for a layperson, at the end of the study in 2010. In addition we will send you a copy of your Y chromosome genetic fingerprint and an explanation sheet designed for the layperson.

In this study we wish to study only unrelated men, so if you know that a male-line relative (e.g. a son or brother) has taken part, unfortunately we will not be able to analyse your DNA.

During this project we are looking at normal variation only, and no targeted tests of any medical consequence are done. However, while analyzing Y-chromosomal variation it can be found, in very rare cases, that a man has lost part of his Y chromosome which is related to fertility. Therefore, if you concerned about the risks of detecting infertility, we would suggest that you do not take part.

Please find enclosed everything you need to take part in the study. Please do not hesitate to contact us at the address or phone numbers above, should you require any further information. We very much look forward to receiving your sample.

Yours sincerely,

Dr. Turi King

January 2009 v.3

From: Jobling, M (Dr.)
Sent: Thursday, January 07, 2010 12:52 PM
To: Peter Starbuck
Subject: RE: Surname Study - Starbuck

Hi Peter,

Hope this is okay. By the way, you look to fall in the main R1a haplogroup.

Best wishes,
Turi

Dr Turi King
Department of Genetics
University of Leicester
Leicester, LE1 7RH

Routine forensic DNA typing allows the identification of close relatives. However, people who share a surname may not be close relatives: indeed, they may share a common ancestor several hundred years ago. Fortunately, there is a piece of our DNA which allows us to trace our same-surnamed relatives, however distantly related. This piece of our DNA is the Y chromosome which, just like a surname, is inherited from father to son. All men who share a surname through a common ancestor can therefore, barring any surname changes or illegitimacy, both of which would result in a different Y chromosome type becoming associated with the surname, be expected to share the same Y chromosome type.

Appendix ii

Peter Starbuck – Genealogy
American Starbucks - Genealogical Research Results

Edward Starbuck
born c.1580 Derbyshire, England
Children:

Edward Starbuck
b.1603 Derbyshire, England
d.4th December 1690, Dover, New Hampshire, America

William Starbuck
b. 1607 Derbyshire, England
d. 1673/74 England

Edward Starbuck married Katherine Reynolds in 1635
Children:

Nathanial Starbuck
b. 1636 Derbyshire – Married Mary Coffin.

Jethro Starbuck
b. 1638 Derbyshire, England d. 1650 (run over by a cart aged twelve)

Sarah Starbuck
b. 1640 Derbyshire, England.
Married William Story, Joseph Austin then Humphrey Austin.

Dorcas
b. unknown – Married William Gayer

Abigail
b. unknown – Married Peter Coffin

British William Starbuck
British Starbucks – Genealogical Research Results

Edward Starbuck   b. 1580 - Draycot, Derbyshire.

William Starbuck   b. 1603 - Shottle, Derbyshire d. 1673/74

Daniel Starbuck   b. 1651 - Shottle, Derbyshire d. 1723

Roger Starbuck   b. 1692 - Shottle, Derbyshire d. 1757

William Starbuck   b. 1721 - Allestree, Derbyshire d. 1798

Charles Starbuck   b. 1745 - Breadsall, Derbyshire d. 1827

Thomas Starbuck   b. 1772 - Breadsall, Derbyshire d. 1856

William Starbuck   b. 1813 - Broughton, Derbyshire d. 1872

Herbert Starbuck   b. 1837 - Morley, Derbyshire d. 1913

Herbert Starbuck   b. 1875 - Ramsbottom, Lancs. d. 1956

Herbert Starbuck   b. 1905 - Darwen, Lancashire d. 1992

Herbert Peter Starbuck b. 1936 - Kingstanding, Birmingham.

Appendix iii

Family Crests/Starbuck's American Coats of Arms

There are differences between the British system and the American system. In Britain the creation and use of heraldry is strictly controlled and has to be approved by the College of Arms.

The American system is less formal and was not clearly understood by the British administrators I consulted. An enquiry to Philip Davies at the British Museum in London proved helpful, leading to further information from Anna Girvan of London's US Embassy, as follows:

> *"In the United States there is no heraldic regulation, and citizens are legally free to adopt whatever arms they wish. While there are no legal restrictions on assuming arms there are however ethical and moral ones. Prior to assuming arms the potential armiger should first find out whether or not a proposed design already belongs to someone else, either currently or in the past. A coat of arms is a graphic representation of the identity of its bearer and to adopt another's arms intentionally or negligently could be considered the moral equivalent of identity theft.*
>
> *While there is less risk of legal consequences in the United States than in some other countries, it can be considered morally wrong. Simply having the same last name as others does not entitle the adoption and use these coats of arms and normally it should be provable there is a direct line of descent from the original armiger to the potential armiger*
>
> *Without evidence of descent from the original armiger, or obtaining their explicit permission, it would be dishonest, disrespectful and misleading for someone to use the original person's arms as their own. Instead, the person who wants arms*

of his or her own should design new arms to represent themselves and their descendants. There are many organizations that Americans can use to assist them in this process."

In Americana Illustrated (vol. XXV, no. 2, 1931: p284) Second Quarter (The American Historical Society Inc.), there is the following entry:

The Starbuck Arms

Argent, a pale gules, bordered azure, between four stars of six points each, of the third. Crest -A raised lion's head.

The surname Starbuck, according to Lower, quoting Ferguson, is derived from the Old Norse, with the following explanation:

> *In the Old Norse, 'bokki' means Vir grandis, corpora et animo. Hence "Storbock I" from "Store, great, vir, imperious".*

The name literally means 'great man or leader' and is first found in English records in the poll take of West Riding, Yorkshire, in 1379.

Bibliography

Books referencing the Starbuck family name.

Herman Melville (1851). *Moby Dick, or The Whale.*

Macy, O. (1880). *The History of Nantucket (1835-80).* Mansfield, Macy & Pratt

Thomas, F. (1920). *The Builders of Milford, Haverfordwest,* The Western Telegraph.

Lubbock, A. (1929). *The Downeasters American Deep Water Sailing Ships* 1869–1929. Glasgow, Brown, Son & Ferguson

Stevens, W. (1936). *Old Nantucket The Farawt Island.* New York, Dodd, Mead & Company.

Gardner, W. (1945). *Three Bricks and Three Brothers.* Cambridge, Mass., Riverside Press.

Rees, J. (1954). *The Story of Milford.* Uni. of Wales Press.

Stackpole, Edward A. (1963) *Nantucket Rebel.* Ives Washburn, Inc

Guba, E. (1965). *Nantucket Odyssey.* Walham, Massachusetts

Loughran, L. (1979). *A Survey of Mercantile House Flags and Funnells* Wolverhampton, Waine Research Publications.

Heffernan, Thomas Farel (1981). *Stove by a Whale.* Wesleyan University Press

Gambee, R. (1986). *Nantucket Island.* New York & London, Norton Co.

Starbuck, A. (1989). *History of The American Whale Fishery* New Jersey, Castle Books.

Abbey, Lloyd (1990). *The Last Whales.* Double Day a division of Transworld Publishers Ltd

Cornwell, Bernard (1995). The Starbuck Chronicles *Battle Flag.* HarperCollins Publishers

Schultz, Howard and Dori Jones Young (1997). *Pour Your Heart Out.* New York, Yang Hyperion.

Philbrick, N. (2000). *In the Heart of the Sea The Epic True Story that Inspired 'Moby Dick'.* London, Harper Collins.

Stephen Harding, Mark Jobling and Turi King (2000). *Viking DNA.* Countryvise Limited and Nottingham University.

Philbrick, Nathaniel (2000). *In the Heart of the Sea.* Harper Collins Publishers

Starbuck, George (2002). *Visible Ink.* The University of Alabama Press

Dolin, Eric Jay (2007). *The History of Whaling in America.* W.W. Norton & Company Limited

Michelli, Joseph. A. (2014). *Leading the Starbucks Way.* McGraw Hill Education

Steve Ashby & Alison Leonard (2018). *Vikings.* Thames & Hudson

The Starbuck Name in History.
The Generations Network Inc., Utah - (ongoing).

About the Author Dr Peter Starbuck

FRICS, FCIOB, FCMI, Ph.D.
Alumni, The Open University
Founding Professor, University Centre Shrewsbury. Visiting Professor, University of Chester as a member of their Business Research Institute, China Centre.

Peter Starbuck is an entrepreneur and academic. He is an acknowledged world expert on Peter F Drucker (1909-2005), the hugely influential Austrian-born management consultant and writer, whose ideas shaped the modern business corporation. Dr Starbuck is an Honorary Member of the Drucker Society – Europe

A successful businessman in the construction industry, he was an adviser to 10 Downing Street on affordable housing. His entrepreneurial endeavours continue to this day as a contributor to non-profit organisations and prolific writer on management concepts.

Peter began reading Drucker's works in detail in 1974, immediately becoming a disciple of his thinking, which was grounded on the same ethical principles he was already practising. Drucker's appeal was that the responsibility of managers and entrepreneurs was to help others. The first responsibility was to those around you, who worked for you, in your organisation. He accumulated a comprehensive understanding of Drucker's ideas and was eventually invited by The Open University to undertake a PhD. on the subject. His supervisor was Professor. Derek S. Pugh the acclaimed writer on management and organisations. Peter was awarded his Doctorate and subsequently his thesis was deposited within the British Library, to date the only one on record from within the British Isles.

He has produced six books on Drucker and is currently working on further material for publication. Frequently asked to contribute material from his vast database and personal knowledge, he has written many articles on the subject of management. Peter has an impressive network of contacts worldwide and attends the annual Drucker Forum in Vienna as an Honorary Member.

Peter Starbuck was born on 5th February 1936 in Birmingham in the heart of the industrial West Midlands. He qualified as a construction professional but his career was interrupted by conscription for National Service in the Corps of the Royal Engineers. Following training in England, he was posted to the British Zone in West Germany from 1959 to 1961 bordering what Winston Churchill dubbed the 'Iron Curtain', erected by the USSR in the Cold War era.

Returning to civilian life, and taking a year to refocus his career, Peter moved to the Welsh-border town of Oswestry, where he developed his construction and house-building business.

For years, Peter and his Welsh wife Heather have enjoyed international travel, mainly to explore the natural world. His ongoing interest is in how it can inform the management thinking of today – using the theme 'How Nature Managed First'.

He firmly believes that nature has important messages through its evolution and designs, many of which have already been subjected to 'Biomimicry'. He has published a book aimed at budding managers that contains many examples of where the natural world has led the way in management and organisation development.

Peter and Heather have two sons, two daughters, grand and great grandchildren.

STARBUCK

Printed in Great Britain
by Amazon